Th[illegible]sons of Youth Work

How to Survive and Thrive for the Long Term

Paul Beautyman
Director of 'Youth Work Journeys'

GROVE BOOKS LIMITED
RIDLEY HALL RD CAMBRIDGE CB3 9HU

Contents

Acknowledgments

Thanks to my editor Tim Gough who encouraged, supported and guided me through this project.

First Impression September 2024
ISSN 1748-3492
ISBN 978 1 78827 417 3

1 Introduction

I chatted recently with a youth worker who said that Christian youth work must never shrink to become merely a youth worker factory. I agree! Christian youth work should be an adventure in loving God, young people and ourselves. However, I also believe one sign of healthy Christian youth work is naturally developing its own leaders. I love seeing young Christians tentatively step into leadership, first-time leaders thrive with more responsibilities and mature leaders nurturing other leaders.

How to sustain and grow Christian youth workers is the purpose of this booklet, rooted in my experience and the lives of people I have been privileged to work with over the years. Sadly, this progression does not happen often enough. This book will show you why, before providing practical steps to help leaders start, grow and flourish through Four Seasons of their career. Enabling Christian youth workers is the aim of my business, 'Youth Work Journeys,' and I would love to have a conversation with you, whether you are a young leader, youth worker, line manager, or trainer. You can contact me on paulbeautyman67@gmail.com and see my work at youthworkjourneys.com

Before we start, I would like to clarify my language: I use the terms 'Christian youth workers' and 'Christian youth work,' but I recognize the differences between Christians doing youth work and youth pastors engaged in youth ministry. For this booklet I will refer to Christian youth work to encompass both.

The Four Seasons of Christian Youth Work

I believe a Christian youth work career usually has Four Seasons. These Four Seasons give us a model that is flexible for supporting the decades-long growth from a young person first going to a youth club, through to them maturing into a Christian youth worker who enables others.

Throughout this booklet, I will share practical guidance to help youth workers, line managers, trainers, and educators provide the correct support, know how to manage expectations and deal with crises throughout each of these Four Seasons.

The Beginning Season

We could call this the 'pre-youth worker' stage. Here a young person (usually but not always) begins going to a youth club and enjoys the activities, makes friends and develops an interest in faith. They are increasingly settled in the values and activities of the club and feel that this Christian youth work is like a home or a family. It is also a time when they take their first steps in leadership.

The Early Season

The 'volunteer youth worker' stage. Imagine someone as part of a group of older teenagers who have grown up through the youth club and are now central to everything that happens, who provide leadership just by being themselves. They start learning more about Christian youth work, probably first in their local club or church, and then in the wider Christian youth work networks they belong to. This might develop into more formal training. Finally, their views and beliefs about the Christian faith and youth work practice which shaped their Beginning Season are now challenged by tasting other Christian experiences or youth work practices, before they test them, possibly as an intern or part-time worker.

The Middle Season

The 'new professional youth worker' stage. There are now several commitments to make: First, after they have worked through the experiences of their Early Season, they must decide what they believe about their Christian faith and Christian youth work practice, committing to these beliefs and letting them shape what they do. They commit to a location or role, probably in their first or second full-time job. On the other side, their new employer or church also commits to them, providing salary, expenses, line management and resources for the youth work to flourish around them.

The Late Season

We might call this the 'experienced professional youth worker' stage. They are often less connected to young people directly, but are developing young leaders, adult volunteers and sometimes staff to grow the youth work instead. This approach can develop as their employers may work in partnership with a Christian youth work agency or parachurch charity, and this gives them more time in a role across a larger area, or they may just start a new job with a much wider facilitation role, but it likely does not involve as much locally-based work.

I am sure these Four Seasons will look familiar to you, either from your own experience or in other Christian youth workers you know, but I do not claim that every Christian youth worker fits neatly into these descriptions. As one youth worker reminded me, 'Labels are for jars not people!' I am convinced, however, that working through this model stage by stage enables the development of fruitful and long-term Christian youth work careers. Doing this can also reduce the number of Christian youth workers who drop out too soon. Therefore, we will use stories to explore these Seasons in more detail throughout the rest of the booklet. We will identify relevant expectations and confirm the impact a person might make in each Season, as well as the specific supports required for them to flourish in whatever Season they are in. We will also discover how moving through the Seasons is not guaranteed just because we get older or are promoted—or even necessary if God calls you to remain in a specific Season. Instead, we will find out how successfully working through what we can call growth spirals can enable a Christian youth worker to mature in their work as they transition through the Seasons.

Myth 1: Short term

Throughout this booklet I want to introduce three destructive myths about Christian youth work that weaken the long-term development of workers. The first is that Christian youth work is short-term. This misunderstanding says proper Christian youth work can be achieved in a few hours a week, and growth should be seen within just a few months, and by just two years miraculous transformations should occur. We all know what pressures this myth creates! This squeezes all the support given to Christian youth workers into a few hours a year, rather than growing over time. The Four Seasons model will show that nurturing Christian youth workers requires significant time, involving days, not hours, and progress should be celebrated over decades not months. I love working with Christian youth workers and saying how I look forward to meeting them ten years later and still involved in Christian youth work!

Reflection Questions

- Which of the Four Seasons do I think I am in?
- What might it take for me to move to the next Season?
- Where have I experienced the 'short term' myth?

2 Role-identity Formation

Before we get into the specific Seasons, we need to look at what I call role-identity formation, an ongoing and dynamic process that drives growth throughout our careers.

A Christian youth worker's career is complex, resembling a forest rather than a single tree. Their work role is not just one tree but rather a seedbed for other roles as they develop within their job. Surrounding these trees is a forest of other trees that symbolizes the Christian youth worker's relationships, health, beliefs, values and even hobbies. Each tree's growth impacts the others, so sustaining a long-term Christian youth work career requires embracing this complexity. Unlike a real forest though, where trees tend to grow uniformly, these metaphorical trees are influenced by shared experiences and actually grow at different rates. For instance, work may be thriving while a personal relationship causes distress, or a crisis of faith may be hidden behind a busy work life. Over the years, these complexities become increasingly interwoven and can lead to conflicts, ultimately hindering a Christian youth worker's ability to continue.

This is where we need role-identity formation. I created this term after listening to experienced Christian youth workers describe how they thrived despite challenges. As one said, it was about, 'figuring out how you work and having space to be you…who God made you to be in your identity.'[1] Youth workers often do not recognize or understand their formation, and the shortage of Late-Season Christian youth workers proves that development is haphazard. The Four Seasons show us the landscape of a Christian youth work career, but role-identity formation enables us to travel through it. Role-identity formation is a lifelong process that integrates a Christian youth worker's work roles and self-identity into a sense of calling. I once asked an experienced Christian youth worker why he had remained despite facing challenges, and he replied, 'This is who I am.' This formation requires a robust and flexible process; robust to cope with the challenges we see in the forest, yet also flexible enough to operate in constantly changing contexts. The impact of this formation is transformational, similar to Richard Rohr's description of initiation, to 'know who you truly are [so] you can hold this fire without burning up and burning out.'[2]

Let us explore the three key elements of *role, identity* and *formation*.

Role

'Role' describes what a Christian youth worker *does*, their job, activities and their outer journeys. They gather skills and information, which then deepen into the committed ownership of a role that can sustain a whole career. This begins with developing existing skills before discovering new abilities, which are then honed and improved. Christian youth work is demanding, though, and a Christian youth worker may turn away from the challenges of learning and maturing in their role. For this, we need to engage in what is known as reflective practice, an intentional process to deepen awareness of what is happening in our roles and then using that to improve. Reflective practice needs us to ask these questions regularly:

- *What?* What happened in a youth work activity?
- *So what?* Why was that significant?
- *Now what?* What should happen next to improve?
- *Who am I becoming?* How should that shape the Christian youth worker I am?

Identity

'Identity' describes who a Christian youth worker *is*: their faith, values, beliefs and inner journeys. Built up in relationships with others, it helps us discover who we are and who we are meant to be, relying heavily on the kind of spiritual formation Henri Nouwen defined as 'the movements from the mind to the heart through prayer in its many forms...[which] reunites us with God, each other and our truest selves.'[3] This is particularly relevant in challenging the busyness of Christian youth workers. Using spiritual disciplines such as prayer, silence, solitude or confession, space is created for God to engage with us, and us with God.[4] This space allows a Christian youth worker to develop their own faith without having simultaneously to carry the full weight of developing the faith of young people. This is challenging as younger workers are expected to lead when their faith is still maturing, and older workers often face significant crises but are not expected to share their struggles. The responsibility for faith sharing and discipleship, however, should be shared by the whole Christian community, not just the youth worker.

Formation

'Formation' is the continual process that integrates a youth worker's role and identity. One week, their reflection on leading a youth club shapes their understanding of their Christian faith. The next week, using a tool like *lectio divina* might alter how they work with volunteers. It is this integration, nurtured by formational mentors in Christian community, that sustains Christian youth workers. Paul Nash's description of an integrative theology for youth work is helpful here, explaining that it 'must invite guests and voices to the discussion table.'[5]

In my own role-identity formation I have often wondered who God was. I have encountered a glorious range of Christian understandings about him. Some focus on Jesus' saving work on the cross, others his commitment to the poor, while others seek to imitate Jesus as incarnate God in their neighbourhood. They describe meeting and serving God in worship services, school chaplaincy, political engagement, counselling or playing games with children. Many would draw on a mix of these and still other Christian beliefs. What they share is being challenged by living out their response to Jesus' call to follow him while building a robust relationship with God. In this they challenge God about the injustices of the world, the pain and distress of a young person's suffering, or the lack of response to the gospel at a summer camp. Their lives are trying to balance the integrity that comes from holding together their Christian faith and the experiences of young people. They are constantly being wonderfully formed and re-formed, but the process is demanding and draining.

Myth 2: Fixed and functional

I now challenge the myth that Christian youth work is fixed and functional, task-based work replicated by running the same prepackaged programmes in different locations. These misunderstandings damage Christian youth workers' support by shrinking it into using books or resources to only improve the functional performance of youth worker in their jobs. Instead, role-identity formation shows us that sustaining youth workers must nurture both their inner and outer journeys where they have time and space to mature within the body of Christ. This is not just a comfort blanket, because wisdom is required to know when self-centredness or a resistance to change must be challenged. We cannot do this work alone.

Reflection Questions

- Do I regularly engage in reflective practice to grow in my role?
- What spiritual disciplines have helped me develop my own faith?
- How do the two of these dialogue in my life to aid my healthy formation?

3

The Beginning Season

This will be our shortest chapter, as it explores the Season *before* someone becomes a Christian youth worker. However, this is also a very important stage that is easily overlooked. So, let me introduce the first of four fictional characters: *Adam*.

Adam is in his first year at high school, has recently started coming to the youth club and gets on well with everyone. All the leaders and young people enjoy his company, and he happily gets involved in everything, especially the games which he enjoys helping other young people to take part in.

He is also worried about his grandad, who has cancer. Nobody at home really talks much about that so he has looked up a lot online but does not feel like he can really talk about it with his friends. The club is usually noisy, and the conversations are always led by one of the leaders on subjects Adam is not really interested in, or about the Bible which he has never read and does not want to. He thinks he might not come back next week.

So we have Adam, who has recently started going to a youth club, enjoys all the activities, feels a real sense of belonging to the group, and a growing connection with the Christian faith, but lots of questions too. We can describe him as a *pre*-youth worker. In this chapter we will explore some practical guidance to help him move through the Season.

We can break each of the Four Seasons into smaller stages, or 'sub-Seasons,' and here we can divide the Beginning Season into *securing* and *starting* sub-Seasons.

Securing

We need to resist looking for leaders too quickly among young people, as focusing on the popular person, or rejecting the troubled or troublesome person is dangerously easy. Instead, we should provide quality Christian youth work for everyone with the emphasis on everyone generously receiving more than they give back. Simply expect that everyone should enjoy being involved and feel secure. Christian youth work should be a good place to be, securing young people by holistically nurturing and celebrating their social, physical, intellectual, emotional and spiritual lives. The impact of these young people will then be in bringing their wonderful energy and enthusiasm to the club.

Starting

The movement between sub-Seasons is subtle and flows back and forth. However, I root the starting of a Christian youth worker's career on what I call the *get it, give it* approach. This means that young people should share what they get. So, if someone gives them a smile, they give a smile back. I gently increase this by, for example, young people setting up and tidying away activities alongside adult volunteers. Here leadership is experienced as service. This Sub-Season usually begins in teenage years, but it can apply to adults too. One Christian youth worker became a Christian in his thirties and immediately started volunteering at his local youth club. Quickly he and others sensed that he should become a Christian youth worker. He underwent training and moved through the Early, Middle and Later Seasons. Most Christian youth workers I have met, however, began their leadership pathway in their early teenage years during this starting period.

Supporting the Beginning Season

When we first met Adam, he was worried about his grandad and was not really connecting with the teaching at his youth group. He did not think he would go back. This is a reminder of the unique challenges every young person faces. Therefore, the support in this Season must focus on the whole person— a holistic care rooted in Christian love and compassion.

We must first listen, learn, and love; *listen* carefully to every young person's story, *learn* what is shaping them and then *love* them generously! In later years, they will lead as they have been led, so regularly receiving love, compassion and forgiveness in this Beginning Season is critical.

Reflection Questions

- What in Adam's story is familiar to me?
- Are there young people in my group like Adam? What do they need?
- What can I do to make sure all young people in my group feel listened to, learned about and loved individually?

4

The Early Season

Aileen is our second fictional youth worker. She is in her final year at high school and is a young leader in her Christian youth project which she has been coming to with her friends since she started high school. She is part of a group who have enthusiastically been involved in everything the project runs and whenever they are involved there is a buzz of excitement, encouraging new teenagers to join and beginning to support adult volunteers and staff.

Instead of going on summer camp as a young leader, however, she wants to travel, see more of the world and explore what different faiths believe. She and her friends are a bit tired of being depended on always to be involved in the youth project and feel taken for granted. Despite respecting the leaders, she finds it hard to tell them her thoughts and now wants to drop out.

Aileen and her friends flourished in their Beginning Season and now bring energy, laughter and depth to all the activities and the ethos of the club. In this chapter, we will explore expectations, impact and support as she grows into a volunteer youth worker, and how to help her move through the stages of this Season. These are the *playing with pals, skilling and training* and *tasting and testing* sub-Seasons.

Playing with Pals

This Sub-Season develops by encouraging young people to be themselves! Activities may help adults connect with young people, but strong peer relationships are the glue that holds Christian youth work together. This reminds us that great Christian youth work is a shared adventure with young people that empowers and enables them. It cannot just be adults imposing their views on young people.

We should expect these young people to take part in review and planning sessions alongside adults, encouraging them to think and contribute. Leadership development slowly grows from here as we intentionally share out leadership tasks. The expectation is not to overburden young people, but to encourage them to serve others in small ways.

I believe that most tasks a leader does can be shared with young people, like leading a small-group discussion, or planning and reviewing a programme. Young people are still young people, though, and we must ensure that the emphasis is on them receiving more than they are giving. We should also allow young people to fail, mess up in their behaviours, and sometimes not turn up when we are relying on them. This is normal and it is more helpful to find out together why they do this, not just to criticize and take the tasks from them. It takes more time (remember the short-term myth?) but it helps everyone to grow.

Although Aileen is not singled out as a leader, she and her peer group make a great contribution just by being themselves. Leadership here is a group function where their positive participation in discussions or activities encourages others to also get involved. We should expect each person to bring their own skills, passions and even problems as these can encourage their friends to come along, refresh activities or shape a discussion.

Skilling and Training

Skilling provides Christian youth work attitudes, skills and knowledge and is given by the church, charity or agency they are a part of. Training, however, dives deeper and draws in wider resources such as Christian youth work networks or higher education. I have also seen adults step into full-time Christian youth work roles after years of being volunteers, so keeping this broad focus is helpful for the long-term development of more Christian youth workers.

By now a dependable level of commitment is expected but needs to be constantly reviewed, rewarded and celebrated. A common question is, 'Do our young leaders need to be Christians?' This is tricky! While running a sports ministry my slogan for young leaders was 'Serious about God, sport and serving others.' We agreed this meant they had to commit to serving other young people, be involved in a sports team and willingly participate in Bible studies without insisting on their belief in the Christian message. I did not want young people saying they were Christians just to become leaders. Some young leaders became Christians and others did not. This separates *leadership* from *discipleship*, where all leaders should be disciples but not all disciples need to become leaders. It is important that Aileen expects to be challenged, as despite her growth she is still a young person to be nurtured. There are usually questions around her relationships with young people as she gets older, so age-appropriate boundaries and safeguarding guidelines need to be constantly reviewed and worked out together.

All leaders should be disciples but not all disciples need to become leaders

Through skilling and training Aileen and her friends should provide a bridge between younger people and adults which can deepen the quality of Christian youth work as stronger relationships are built and better communication enabled. Impact will mainly be seen among young people close to Aileen, but the impact will also be irregular or inconsistent, so avoid expecting too much of her. For wider and more sustained impact we will need to wait until the Middle Season.

Tasting and Testing

In my experience this is an awkward Sub-Season for the Christian youth worker and everyone around them as the volunteer youth worker matures into a new professional youth worker (Middle Season, chapter five). This is like a leaving home moment, when their church or leadership encourages the person to leave what is familiar to them and taste different approaches to youth work and the Christian faith. They might go to college to study Christian youth work or move to another church. These new ideas must then be tested by the person, weighing what sustains them through the widening challenges of Christian youth work they are facing. There may be a return to the places, practices and beliefs that nurtured them, or they may adopt new practices. What is more important is that their beliefs and practices are now robustly owned by them, and not merely accepted out of loyalty to the leaders and Christian communities that raised them.

While they are still in training and not a qualified Christian youth worker, we should move towards a balance of giving and getting, where the person is still supervised and supported but also has meaningful responsibilities. This requires dependable commitment from them to attend and prepare for activities, and for them to be willing to learn, and also be expected to engage critically with leadership. I would also suggest that by now a clear Christian faith is required.

By now their impact should be consistently increasing, for longer times with more people across wider areas of work than in the playing with pals or skilling and training sub-Seasons. Through their practice and questions, their involvement should raise standards, providing new resources and insights in Christian faith and youth work practice.

Supporting the Early Season

Character always comes first, so showing and sharing the Christian faith must lie at the core of compassionate pastoral care. Then we need to remember that peer relationships are not always easy, and we need to be ready to help groups love and heal. Next, we constantly involve them, encouraging them to discover their views and share them with other young people and leaders. All this is best wrapped into a recognized young leaders' pathway. This is not easy work, as every Christian youth worker knows, so the leader of these young people also needs support and advice, constantly to renegotiate age-boundaries, avoid favouritism, and bring a constant readiness to forgive.

As they move through the sub-Seasons, additionally leadership development should be modelled on an apprentice system of what I call, *I do, we do, you do*. They start by watching, then by joining in, and then get to try things on their own. Within this should come opportunities to explore if a youth work career is for them.[6] Again, support for adult leaders is required, especially in managing the difficult transition from working with Aileen as a young person and then as a colleague.

I think it is important to begin with what the leader of this developing youth worker needs. Letting go of a young person in whom we have invested so much, and possibly now rely on, is challenging. We must address our own sadness or disappointments and seek advice and introductions to other Christian youth work networks. If we handle this well, the transition between Seasons succeeds, inspiring other young people to follow Aileen and expanding the pool of potential Christian youth workers. Aileen's leader may also progress into their next sub-Season themselves! However, if we get it wrong, neither Aileen nor her leader will advance, and the pathway for other young people will be lost. Everyone loses.

For Aileen, she needs a place to be honest about her growing questions about her faith and practice. This might be in the youth work tribe she grew up in, but it is also helpful to find people among the networks she is exploring. Look back to Aileen's playing with pals sub-Season, and how we encouraged them to find their own voice and share their views with leaders. Look back to how the adult leaders increasingly made space to listen, learn and love. Those tentative steps equip everyone for these trickier conversations. As we finish this Season, remember Aileen not wanting to go on summer camp but wanting to explore and finding it difficult to share this with the leaders? If we help her through these sub-Seasons, she will be ready to leave home but not leave Christian youth work, and so mature into the Middle Season.

Reflection Questions

- Which young people have we released into greater responsibilities?
- Do we provide opportunities for these young leaders to grow and learn?
- How could we help these young leaders try their strengths and test new ideas?
- When do we need to let go of these young leaders so that they can grow beyond us?

The Middle Season

5

Tom is our next fictional youth worker. He is new in town and has a growing reputation as an excellent pastor of young people and an engaging speaker at youth events. He also has a dynamic approach to running residential camps, where he is a leader with a Christian youth work agency. The local churches have invested heavily in him by working together to raise funds.

However, despite the outward appearance of success, Tom is struggling. He feels out of his depth, having rushed towards this opportunity when he was actually more settled in the church where he had grown up and become a Christian. Tom had volunteered there while studying at university, and took on sessional youth work in the holidays when term ended. The network around him during his volunteer and sessional times helped him to work through his tasting and testing sub-Season when he was still in his Early Season. Tom now owns his own Christian beliefs and youth work practices, which should enable him to flourish in this new Season. Unfortunately, the challenges of this new role are overwhelming him, and his training has not equipped him for these tasks—especially leading volunteers who are mostly older than him. Many of Tom's volunteers have stepped back, feeling unnecessary since his hiring, leaving him more isolated.

As a result, he feels unprepared and scared, even though he is having a significant impact on the young people, volunteers, churches, and communities he is involved with as a new professional youth worker. Tom is thinking of going back to university to study to become a teacher instead.

Tom is now ready to mature into the *mark-making* and *mutual-commitment* sub-Seasons as a new professional youth worker. There is a big red-flag warning here though! Of all the transitions, this is the one most likely to deceive us with superficial appearances. Tom will not enter this Season simply because he has a Christian youth work job (often his first), with an impressive title and maybe even his own office. He will only truly enter this Season when someone helps him to healthily work through the outstanding stages of previous Seasons.

Mark-making

The first expectation we should look to meet in this Season is becoming a Christian youth worker who is both robust and flexible. A robust youth worker faces situations and issues they have not experienced before by drawing on resources in their faith and practices. A flexible youth worker can access and adopt new practices, and will adapt to developing needs. A robust and flexible Christian youth worker knows when they need to be robust or flexible! The ability to work like this while growing will enable Tom to make his mark and become a dynamic and unique youth worker.

If the Christian youth worker is not robust but *rigid*, and not flexible but *floppy*, then something needs addressing. Rigid is when someone cannot or will not explore any belief, idea or practice that is different from what they grew up with or already know. Floppy is the exact opposite, as they always go with the latest idea they hear about. Neither approach will let them make their mark as a growing Christian youth worker.

I would expect a healthy Christian youth work in this Season consistently to be able to describe, enable and achieve success. Success in Christian youth work is a controversial subject! Do we measure it in numbers, commitments, counselling sessions or specific conversation topics? Whatever the definition, it needs to be agreed in discussion with young people, volunteers, staff and wider project leadership, and then it needs to be regularly assessed, learned from and celebrated when achieved.

Success in Christian youth work is a controversial subject!

I tell Christian youth workers that if they hit all their targets, the targets were probably too easy, but if they hit less than a quarter, the targets were too tough. To achieve success, we need thoughtfully to integrate understanding of success and targets into our work with volunteers and young leaders, ensuring that our Christian faith and resources grow together. As in previous Seasons, the Christian youth worker is deeply involved in every aspect of the work, but now the ripples of growth regularly extend beyond them, impacting more young people through the efforts of young leaders, adult volunteers, and staff.

Mutual Commitment

Mutual commitment is double-sided. On one side, the Christian youth worker who has worked through the previous sub-Seasons (especially the tasting and testing sub-Season) now commits to particular Christian beliefs and practices and roots them into a place and people in a church or project. On the other side, that place and people commit to the youth worker themselves, providing resources, salary and support for them to flourish.

I mentioned earlier how all sub-Seasons flow around each other. They are not always linear, so a person does not always progress neatly from one to another. This is particularly true of the mark making and mutual commitment sub-Seasons as they often overlap. Sometimes the mark-making occurs because of the prior mutual commitment to a Christian youth worker by their church. Sometimes this mutual commitment grows out of the Christian youth worker's mark-making which opens up possibilities and prepares for growth. Whatever the order, they are both required.

During this sub-Season, the youth worker should now be carrying real responsibilities. This requires them to operate from out of both their gifts *and* skills. Gifts are the natural and God-given aspects of their character: who they naturally are. Remember back in chapter three, how Adam enjoyed being part of the club, and how it nurtured his entire holistic life? Or remember how Aileen and her friends in chapter four developed leadership by just being themselves? Those early experiences helped uncover and affirm their God-given gifts and that was enough at that time. However, through skilling and training, and tasting and testing from the Early Season, the volunteer youth worker should develop the wider skills required to become a professional here in this Season. I confess my frustration when I meet youth workers who say something like, 'I love young people but can't work with parents or adult volunteers,' or those who half-joking admit, 'I love working with young people but I'm rubbish at planning.' I have learned that my frustration is not really with them, but with the training, support and management structures that have allowed them to only operate with their gifts. Sadly, too many people with these responsibilities do not know what skills are required, nor do they know how to access the training available to gain those skills. Sometimes, their employers are unwilling to invest the money to provide this training for them. This is a central reason why so much Christian youth work does not flourish.

In the mark-making sub-Season we should expect success regularly to ripple outwards from the youth worker into a widening group of people and events. This success should be varied and deeply impact the lives of young people, while also extending broadly into the leadership decisions of church and surrounding communities. In this sub-Season the impacts of a church and youth worker mutually committing to each other create what a friend once described as 'fruit tree growth.' This does not happen immediately after the seed or sapling is planted, but rather when the tree matures and is repeatedly nurtured in the right soil. Then we can expect fruit every Season.

Supporting the Middle Season

In any Season I believe every Christian youth worker needs to pay their bills, save money and live well while also investing in their future. They require fair terms and conditions, opportunities for development and skilled line-management rooted in the pastoral care of a Christian community. As commitments are mutually made to each other by a youth worker and church, these are increasingly important as the youth worker grows into larger responsibilities, maybe including a family or a mortgage. It is depressingly common for

Christian youth workers either not to enter this Season or to leave too soon after starting, as they cannot afford to live within it.

Professionally, peer mentoring is important for a Christian youth worker to continue developing their skills, especially around leadership. I am convinced that it is also helpful to be involved with Christian youth workers from different Seasons, supported by mentors. This helps nurture everyone by developing pathways and strengthening relationships.

These networks can become safe and sacred places where Christian youth workers can bring their own questions and struggles. This needs to be distinct from line management and separate from their public presence in the church. I have often observed that while line management and support for outer journeys continues through a career, pastoral support for inner journeys decreases over time. I think this is based on a belief that older workers, unlike teenagers or young adults, have worked out life and are doing ok. As an older Christian youth worker, however, I know that is not true! We still experience crises of faith and are often increasingly involved with death and disappointments. I have heard people in this position described as the 'sandwich generation,' or people stuck in the middle and caring for their children and teenagers on one side and elderly parents on the other. That is a lot of pressure that needs compassionate and wise pastoral care.

The employer now has a complex task, to provide human resources support, line management, professional training and pastoral care. Few churches or agencies are equipped to do all of this, so it is wise to buy into services from outside. There is a risk of the employee having too many bosses, so it is important for employer and employee mutually to agree and sustain open communication in a dependable but flexible support structure.

Reflection Questions

- Do I recognize myself in this Season?
- What do I need to thrive as a Christian youth worker right now?
- How could I connect with, support and receive support from those around me?

6 The Late Season

Gillian is our last fictional youth worker. She is a well-known Christian youth worker who has worked in the same church and community for years. She is well connected and has supported many young people through difficult times. Some have become Christians, while many adults in the community still chat to her about how they used to love going to the youth club when they were teenagers. She is widely involved in youth work networks and is relied on by younger staff and volunteers for support and advice.

However, under her happy smile, Gillian feels discouraged. Despite her experience, she is rarely involved in leadership conversations in her church. She feels isolated from young people as she now has responsibility for fund-raising and managing teams. She also has an aging mum in a care home several hours' drive away. This takes up much of her time outside work and the travel costs are eating away her savings. She is uncertain if she will continue in Christian youth work but does not know what else to do.

Gillian is effective, busy and in demand, and we could describe her as an experienced professional youth worker. However, she also has significant family pressures, is distanced from leadership decisions in the church, and is uncertain if she will continue. In this chapter we will explore how to help Gillian move through her enabling locally and enabling beyond sub-Seasons.

Enabling Locally

Remember that Gillian will only be ready to flourish in this Season if she has secured the maturing growth in her Middle Season. A worker does not arrive at the Late Season after a certain number of years or receive it as a promotion or reward. They only reach it after demonstrating their ability to nurture and enable fruit tree growth—the kind that grows others.

A worker can remain in the Middle Season for many years if they receive strong support and are not called or nurtured into the Late Season. Perhaps God wants to keep them closer to face-to-face work with young people, for instance? Beware, also, of drawing a worker like Gillian into a wider enabling role if the move masks burnout that is unacknowledged by her or her supporters.

Enabling Beyond

You can see how transitions between Seasons actually get trickier later in a Christian youth work career. Gillian's impacts during this Season can be significant as larger teams grow around her, and everything begins to depend less on her being present. As a leader, she is still aware of all that is happening through strong pastoral care for her team leaders, integrated into excellent line management. The result is growth in areas where the leader is absent, along with a multiplication of groups, activities, and discipleship that nurtures the Beginning, Early and Middle Seasons of other leaders. Leaders are finally growing leaders!

Supporting the Late Season

'The experienced leader takes as much help as possible.' I heard this late on in my career and it has really helped me. Let us not imagine it is only in the Beginning, Early or even Middle Season that a Christian youth worker needs support and advice. Workers like Gillian need time and space to prepare how to equip others, drawing on resources that are constantly being renewed.[7] Alongside this outer work, there is important inner work to be facilitated. Everyone is different but this work can include developing the humility to serve others, dealing with the guilt of possibly working less anti-social hours than others, or the loss of identity from no longer working face to face with young people. Developing rhythms of role-identity formation that are supported by formational mentors and the Christian community in earlier Seasons will again bear fruit here.

It is critical that Christian youth workers like Gillian are still supported. Otherwise, who will mentor the mentor? I know that peer mentoring in this Season has helped me, as well as being connected into networks that include youth workers from all Seasons. I always advise them to keep connected with young people too, even in a limited way, as this is an important source of refreshment. Remember to avoid the 'isolated' myth (see Myth 3, chapter seven) and help Late-season Christian youth workers find their place in Christian communities where they do not always lead youth work and can simply be nurtured as growing Christians.

Reflection Questions

- Do I know a Late-season youth worker? Is it me?
- What are the biggest needs in the Late Season? How do we ask for them?
- What do I need to do now?
- Who do I need to talk with?

Growth Spirals

7

The Four Seasons model shows that if we expect the right growth, and nurture that growth according to each sub-Season, then each Season provides an expanding range of impact and opportunities. Before we leave, I want to emphasize that progression within and between Seasons is not necessarily improvement, where the Season after is necessarily better than the previous one. Instead, we are called to discover and become the person God is calling us to be now, exactly where we are. Progression is also not guaranteed, dependent on age or years in service, or getting promoted. It is only powered by the long, slow, and sometimes painful process of role-identity formation. Finally, progression is not automatic but depends on navigating growth spirals which will be explained in this final chapter.

In the Four Seasons, progression into the next Season is never automatic. Moving into a new Season requires a growth spiral, or a transforming experience of four inner movements: *receiving, breaking, creating* and *settling*. The *receiving* movement provides stability which is fractured by the *breaking* movement. The *creating* movement is the subsequent work of reflection, discovering options and building new approaches to our faith or practice. In the *settling* movement these approaches are integrated into our life and work and the leadership structures that surround us. Growth spirals can repeat, have no fixed time, and can develop maturity within a Season or lead into another.

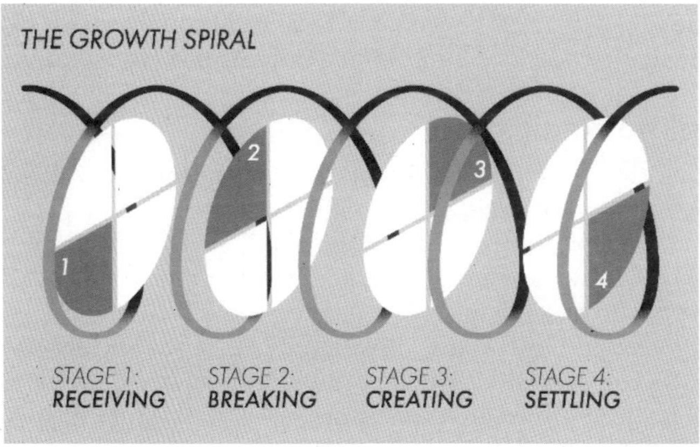

(Image: Ben Mizen)

This looks fairly simple, right? However, our growth in real life is always messier than any model; according to Rohr, 'We are approximately one-third nature, one-third nurture and one-third free choice.'[8] Working through growth Spirals is challenging work, so it is not surprising that many of us do not mature through our Seasons. I will illustrate this by sharing four examples from my own life, although I did not fully understand or even notice them at the time. The first two examples show how I developed between Seasons, and the following two how I matured within a Season.

My Early to Middle Season

This growth spiral took eight years, maturing me from a volunteer into a new professional youth worker.

The *receiving* movement were my years as a summer mission volunteer, running holiday clubs for the Church of Scotland, starting as an inexperienced teenager but developing my skills before becoming a team leader. I made friends, grew in my Christian faith and attended training that resourced me and encouraged me to contribute my views. The *breaking* movement began when I realized traditional models of holiday clubs failed to reach most young people and that the organization's leadership did not offer advice, resources or even see the problem. Tentatively stepping into a *creating* movement, I decided not to accept the organization's approaches but started designing and leading new models of youth work. These successfully engaged more young people with experiences of the Christian faith and encouraged me that I could critique existing Christian youth work practice and make my own contribution. The formation of my faith, confidence, skills and knowledge in this creating movement led into my *settling* movement where I got my first Christian youth work job, organizing the summer mission programme. In this instance, my growth spiral was enabled externally, in the rambling development pathway provided by the church's training structures for volunteers.

Responding to a Crisis

The previous growth spiral matured me over eight years, but this one changed me in a few hours. My *receiving* movement was being rooted in a job planting a church for young people and their families in Edinburgh. I had been a Christian youth worker for 15 years, contributed nationally and now led this innovative project. All was well. However, my secure youth work world was about to crash. The *breaking* movement began at a review meeting, in a heated discussion with the panel about values and approaches. Eventually the review leader claimed that this project was not a church, and I was not the leader it required. I left the session bruised and battered and wandered down to the high school. There, I slumped in the PE staffroom, feeling sorry for myself and moaning about the review. The staff were not Christians, but they gently reminded me of my role as a rugby coach, affirming my pastoral care of staff and students as their school chaplain, including officiating the weddings of several of their colleagues. In this healing conversation the *creating* movement began, affirming my instinct to work at the edges and discovering these edges were also my sustaining places. This approach was different to most youth workers I knew but it felt right to me. Later I remembered a talk from my supervisor on Ephesians 4 and I realized that I was called by God to be more apostolic in my approach, and that I should grow my youth work alongside youth workers, ministers and volunteers who were prophets, evangelists, shepherds and teachers. This insight about my role identity became a *settling* movement and grounded me for the next 15 years of my career. Unlike the first growth spiral, I was very aware of working through significant changes in my self-understanding and views on youth work, but it did not immediately move me into another Season. Instead, I settled into my Middle Season with a conviction of the person God was shaping me to be. He was encouraging me to share my convictions about Christian youth work despite many challenges.

Going on Retreat

My first growth spirals were reactive, but this one was proactive. My *receiving* movement was an established life rhythm of rest, youth work, preparation and prayer. The *breaking* movement was a decision to leave these typical routines and go on retreat regularly. In the *creating* movement I introduced different rhythms; one hour blocks of prayer, *lectio divina* Bible meditations, silence, reading and meeting my spiritual director. In one retreat I realized that this was who I was, and that these retreats should not just be an annual exception to how I lived as a busy youth worker, but that should define me. So, in a *settling* movement, I began integrating these rhythms into my work. I continued with our noisy and loud youth programmes, but alongside them I introduced quieter reflections and silence—and was amazed to find that young people loved these times too! This growth spiral secured how God nurtured me, shaping my practice and sustaining me. This allowed me to thrive in my Middle Season.

The Gift of a God Whisper

This growth spiral came as a surprising gift. I had been a Christian youth worker for 25 years and my *settling* movement was a regular rhythm of work, reflection and prayer. The *breaking* movement occurred while driving when I heard a voice inside me say, 'Released into life.' It was unsought and not remembered from a song or sermon, so I recognized it as one of the few

God whispers in my life. The *creating* movement then lasted several years as I reflected on what it meant, talking with friends, journaling, praying and starting my PhD. Eventually my wife and I agreed it meant leaving my paid role with the Church of Scotland. This was challenging. It meant leaving a role I mostly enjoyed and felt fulfilled in. Also, I worked with a great group of young people, volunteers and staff. It was hard to think of leaving them. I was also a dad with young children, and walking away from a regular salary without having any job to move into felt precarious. The *settling* movement followed as I matured into the Late Season of my career. During this time I started my own business, 'Youth Work Journeys,' which supports, mentors and trains Christian youth workers. This enabling approach had begun years before in my mark-making sub-Season as I trained young leaders, volunteers, and staff. However, this growth spiral secured my transition into a role where enabling others defined me. I still miss contact work with young people, but the Late Season of my career has begun and I look forward to the future!

Myth 3: Isolated

The last myth is that Christian youth work is isolated, or the youth work functions apart from the whole Christian community. This may be designed by the leadership, inherited by church tradition, or reinforced by a youth worker who holds young people too tightly around them. This approach shapes and damages the nurture of Christian youth workers. Additionally, Christian youth workers only meet other Christian youth workers at conferences, and support networks only connect Christian youth workers. This limits the resources that might sustain us, as well as our experience of God. This approach also weakens the whole Christian community as it loses out on the insightful contribution of Christian youth workers. The growth spirals I have chosen show that my formation is woven in and around other people: the volunteers, staff, family, church leaders, academics and of course, young people that make up the whole people of God. Eugene Peterson said that 'Jeremiah was named and immersed in names…God is as real to a prophet as his next-door neighbour and his next-door neighbour is a vortex in which God's purposes are being carried out.'[9] This relational work weaves around formational mentors based in Christian communities and experienced colleagues who are aware of their own inner and outer journeys and are committed to enabling this formation in others. They can help Christian youth workers draw out meaning or significance so they can grow by humbly remaining in one Season and deepening their resources within it or by riskily moving forward into a new Season.

Reflection Questions

- What Season and sub-Season am I in?
- What do I need in this Season?
- Do I recognize growth spirals in my life?

8 Conclusion

Expect More

Well, there you have it: how to sustain Christian youth workers across Four Seasons of their career.

I think we have all met people like Gillian, Tom, Aileen and Adam. Maybe we even see something of ourselves in them or remember what it was like when we were in their shoes. Remember Jesus saying that the kingdom of God was like a mustard seed, where that small seed grows into a huge bush and many birds find rest in it? That is a lovely image of a developing youth work career: one that starts small but contains the DNA to grow and mature into a place of blessing and shelter for many. Sadly, far too few Christian youth workers mature into Gillian's role, the role which is critical in creating the contexts for Tom, Aileen and Adam to flourish. You will probably be familiar with some of the barriers or obstacles preventing Adam or Aileen from growing into Tom's experience, or those which keep Gillian from remaining, with her youth work flourishing around her.

If I had to sum this up, I would take a risk and say expect more of Christian youth workers. I do not mean for us to work longer hours and take on an ever-increasing list of tasks beyond our remit. That is just the quick way to damaging burnout and helps no one. I mean that when we help Christian youth workers mature through their Seasons, our expectations of them should become wider and deeper. My experience and research show that we should not accept a youth worker's career will last just a few years, nor should they only lead simple activities. Instead, if we invest more in them, we can expect more from them.

I want to see Christian youth workers who are:

- not just better trained, but involved in shaping and delivering training courses, while still youth workers;
- not just better led, but informing and enabling leadership decisions, while still youth workers;
- not just better resourced but creating new resources for the Christian faith and practice, while still youth workers;

- not just better practitioners but engaged in sense-making to create theologically robust insights for the whole people of God, while still youth workers.

I love the insight of Andrew Root into Dietrich Bonhoeffer. Bonhoeffer is well known as a theologian, writer, pastor or even a spy and martyr, but Root understands Bonhoeffer as a youth pastor who had 'young people on his mind,' when he began what Root terms the theological turn in youth ministry.[10] Root describes Bonhoeffer's encounter with a young person in crisis which forced him 'to be nimble, to be a true theological thinker.'[11] I am convinced that when we get role-identity formation right, then every Christian youth worker would develop in this way. OK, we may not all become world famous theologians, but I know that when we expect more, God's life flourishes. Then we will truly become like that mustard seed.

Contact me anytime; I would love to help you or a Christian youth worker you know to journey through these Four Seasons.

Notes

1 P Beautyman. PhD Research ('How role-identity formation sustains Christian youth workers across four seasons of their careers' through the University of Glasgow, 2024) interviewee.

2 R Rohr, *Adam's Return: The Five Promises of Male Initiation* (Redwood City, CA: PublishDrive, 2004) p 161.

3 H Nouwen, *Spiritual Formation: Following the Movements of the Spirit* (San Francisco, CA: HarperOne, 2010) p xvi.

4 For more on this see N Foster, *The Making of an Ordinary Saint: My Journey from Frustration to Joy with the Spiritual Disciplines* (Grand Rapids, MI: Baker Books, 2014).

5 P Nash, *What Theology for Youth Work?* (Grove Youth booklet Y 8) p 27.

6 I recommend C Curtis, A Wilson and K Wilson, *Journey into Youth Work: Discovering Your Call to Work with Young People* (Grove Youth booklet Y 30).

7 I particularly highlight A Campbell, J Osborn and S Nash, *Keys to Well-being in Youth Ministry* (Grove Youth booklet Y 73); N Roberts and L Fox, *Surviving and Thriving: How to Sustain a Calling in Youth Work* (Grove Youth booklet Y 38) and S Nash and J Whitehead, *Ten Essential Concepts for Christian Youth Work* (Grove Youth booklet Y 40).

8 Rohr, *Adam's Return, op cit,* p xii.

9 E Peterson, *Run with the Horses: The Quest for Life at its Best* (Westmont, IL: IVP, 2019) p 26.

10 A Root, *Bonhoeffer as Youth Worker: A Theological Vision For Discipleship and Life Together* (Ada, MI: Baker Academic, 2014) p 68.

11 *ibid,* p 67.